Scenes of Childhood

A Forest of Dean Childhood Remembered
By Bernard Kear

To the memory of Our Mam, Our Dad and Our Thynt.

Published 1992 by
Thornhill Press Limited
24 Moorend Road, Cheltenham, Glos

©Bernard Kear

Printed in England by A.M.C.L. Design and Print.

ISBN. 0 946328 44 7

Contents

Introduction

Bounded by the Severn and Wye, the Forest of Dean was until recent years, a relatively isolated part of Britain. Even as late as the 1939 - 45 war, the Forest was a backwater, its people parochial by nature and distinctly suspicious of outsiders. Most local men laboured in the coal mines and, after emerging at the end of the shift, tended large gardens. Many families kept fowls and a pig, or ran a few sheep in the woods. Like most Foresters our large family lived in a small two-bedroomed cottage with no electricity or water supply.

Following the death of Our Mam in 1940, Our Dad was strongly urged to send us all off to various childrens' homes, but he was a determined man and resolved to keep us together. Relatives and neighbours helped in many ways, but it was to be almost a year before reliable full-time help arrived.

The drawings in this book were completed over several years. They illustrate some of the things we did during our childhood. Friends and relatives suggested they would form an interesting collection if a few lines of explanation were added to each picture. Older people will recognise many of the features of life fifty years ago, while younger people may be astonished as to how much life has changed since those days.

I wish to thank my brothers and sisters for their ideas and criticisms, aunts and uncles for their contributions and my wife for her suggestions and patience. I also wish to thank all those who gave us real help when we needed it most, and offer the work in grateful tribute to Our Mam, Our Dad and Our Thynt.

Taters and Greens

There's nothin' like a gyarden t' give thee vittles t' yut, flowers t' marvel at . . . . an' backache.

Grancher Kear, who was a good gardener, had an enormous influence on our family and little went on that he knew nothing about. He was a knowledgeable man with a forceful character and, having a strong social conscience, took an active interest in Politics, trade Unionism and Methodism.

Grancher has a couple of pieces of string, known as 'yarks', tied around his trouser legs making the knees slightly baggy. He had been a miner and they were worn in the pits. They allowed a sweating man to move more easily by preventing his trousers sticking to his legs, thus putting less strain on braces and buttons. They also helped to stop the dirt going too far up the legs.

Grancher Kear liked a good scratch, especially his back, but could never seem to find the seat of the irritation. He often asked me to scratch where his own hands couldn't reach, but try as I might, I rarely found the right spot. Perhaps the essential feature of an itch is that when the site has been located it moves.

Grancher Kear, "Up a bit, down a bit, more, left, left, harder, come on harder. An' when y' d' get wum tell youer feyther t' find a 'at t' put on yer yud."

In contrast to Grancher's intimidating character, Granny Kear was a tolerant and cheerful little lady. She was quiet and calm but possessed the fortitude to cope with the drudgery that she and other women of her generation had to face. Granny was courageous too. When I was five years of age, a huge sow maddened by milk fever attacked me. It chased me around a patch of gorse and the awful snorting and grizzling noises it made became more and more urgent as it got closer. Froth from its slavering mouth splashed over my legs when my screams of terror alerted Granny who rushed across the green to snatch me from the pig's jaws.

Granny always wore a long plain apron over a dark dress and her hair was gathered into a bun. We visited her on Sunday morning after Sunday school, when she was preparing dinner. We loved to watch her basting meat, preparing vegetables and expertly chopping mint. Of course, like all grannies, she would ask us if we wanted a drink. Granny introduced us to cabbage water, insisting that it was good for us. I am sure she was correct in her assertion; anyway we certainly enjoyed it, thinking it a great treat.

Granny Kear, "If thee 'ast got that mint my mon we ull goo an'
chop it up."

7

It is not in the nature of most children to volunteer readily for any job around the home. However, Our Den was old enough to be aware of the enormous amount of work required to satisfy the many needs of our family and it was not unusual for him to get on with tasks in the garden without being asked. Three of my brothers are not in the picture though; they could be working elsewhere of course, but they have probably got out of the way to avoid being given a job. I wasn't sensible enough to do the same, so as soon as Our Dad spots me in the plum tree he will have something ready for me to do. The girls didn't work on the garden, they helped in the cottage, but they should have known better than to play in the garden with a ball when Our Dad was around.

Dad, "Daaze youer eyes you little martal, get off that gyarden. I 'a' just hoed them taters up. I ull trim youer feathers fer you y' young hussy. Play outside ull y'."

There was plenty to be done on our large garden and there were many times throughout the year when we all worked on it together.

Foresters had a lot of practical gardening knowledge. Generations of delving in coal mines and quarries told them where local rock strata outcropped, while good down-to-earth gardening know-how told them which vegetables best suited each area. To achieve the very best crops seed potatoes were exchanged between friends living on different types of soil. Certain jobs had to be done by particular dates, and for good reasons, e.g. kidney beans were sown on 12th May as this was the earliest date that would ensure their survival through late frosts. Real efforts were made to sow seeds and set out plants during the waxing of the moon. More sophisticated gardeners might feel such considerations to be naive but could not argue with the quality or quantity of the vegetables we harvested.

Dad, *"Thee bist a bit of a token mind, 'tyunt no good thinkin' thee bis' gwain t' clate off yet. Thou const get t' other spitter an' turn thic other pane o' ground over."*

Although we tended a small but colourful flower knot, by far the larger part of our garden was given over to growing vegetables. We helped Our Dad keep the plot in good condition, spreading sheep dung to increase fertility, hoeing regularly to keep the weeds down and liming to maintain the soil in good heart. A healthy plant is less likely to suffer from pests and diseases, even so, we found the caterpillars on the cabbage leaves troublesome. We picked them off by hand dropping them into a jar of lime. It was much more fun though to chase the butterflies, beating them down with pea sticks. Blackfly on the broad beans was another problem. During the summer we saved our old soapy water in the tin bath and Our Dad modified a bike pump so that it could be used as a sprayer. Not many garden pests survived a good dousing with our dirty bath water.

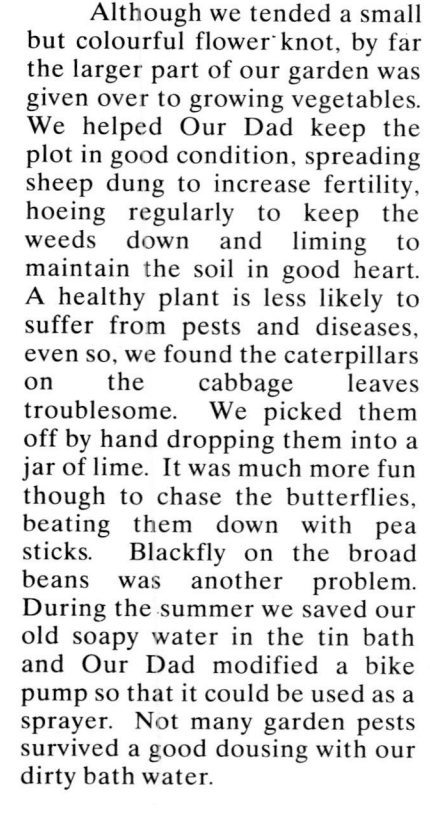

Ger, "Kip thee yud down Our Den."

In order to maintain a fruitful garden, cultivation alone is not enough. Our Dad believed in the use of plenty of 'muck'. Though our pigs and poultry supplied a certain amount, we were regularly sent out in search of more.

Sometimes we took a couple of buckets, at other times we took the big trolley. Usually we took a wheelbarrow, after all we had three of various sizes to choose from; we were the only three-wheelbarrow family in the district.

Often we pushed our barrows miles into the forest to shovel up a worthwile load Our Dad had spotted earlier.

A number of horses wandered around the area sometimes and grazed on the open greens, but as boys, we relied a good deal on Mr. Lowe's horse. Mr. Lowe was our milkman, so we knew his daily round. Moreover, the laws of nature decreed that somewhere along the route, given time, his horse would produce a dollop or two.

The milkman an' 'is hoss.

11

Almost all the dung we collected was from the numerous sheep that wandered freely in the woods and on the greens. These 'Welsh tats', a hardy breed, are still 'run' by local men known as 'ship badgers'. We kept an eye on their movements and where they spent the night; the knowledge would save us time. Sometimes the sheep would be grazing in Cut 'n Fry green, at other times at the edge of the Aisne.

We learnt to use a certain amount of cunning when gathering dung. When Our Dad sent us out to get a barrow 'full' of muck we daren't go home with less. Yet, if we did return with a full load he assumed there must be plenty about so he would send us out again. Our strategy therefore was to put poor quality stuff on top, with bits of stick or grass - anything to give the impression that there was a shortage of dung and we had found it difficult to find enough to fill the barrow.

Pug, "We 'a' got a yup 'ere mon, le's goo wum. I've had a bellyful o' this."

Our plot was large and intensively cropped yet we could never grow enough potatoes on it to meet our needs. One of the local farmers allowed Our Dad to grow several rows in one of his fields. A tractor was used to make the furrows, then Our Dad showed us younger children how to set the tubers and gave us a short stick to space them with. My older brothers were given the job of carrying sacks of taters and filling in the trenches.

Later, when it was time to harvest the crop, Our Pug would look forward to taking the day off school to dig them out. On one occasion the farmer, who happened to be working in the same field, saw Our Pug forking out the taters and volunteered to run the bouting plough down the rows to get them out and save him a lot of hard work. Always keen to demonstrate what he could do and despite the fact that the rows added up to about a third of a mile or more, Our Pug, letting his enthusiasm overcome his common sense, quickly rejected the offer saying, "I ull soon knock these vyow out."

"Another seventeen roots an' I'll 'ave a drink o' pop."

We rubbed most of the dirt off the potatoes then stored them in our top shed. A bed of dried bracken kept them off the stone floor; more bracken and sacks being placed on top. The taters were handled with great care to avoid damage which would eventually lead to decay. Several times during the winter nights we checked the crop to throw out those which were rotting. The large running sore of a putrefying potato is easily recognised and Our Dad would leave me in the silence of the shed to get on with the job alone. As a child I found it an extremely spooky place to work. I often looked over my shoulder, half expecting to be confronted by some ill-intentioned apparition. The shed was inexplicably cold too, even during the summer, and had a strange, damp, musty smell. The small window was densely shrouded in cobwebs and half hidden by boxes and tins full of an odd assortment of objects that 'might come in useful one day'. It was not the sort of place one would spend more time in than one had to.

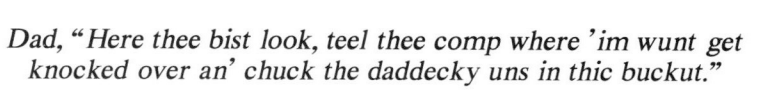

Dad, "Here thee bist look, teel thee comp where 'im wunt get knocked over an' chuck the daddecky uns in thic buckut."

After spending much of the day working with the pigs, the fowls, or in the garden, we sat down to Saturday tea. Often there was little on the table to eat but whatever there was 'had' to be consumed. It was not considered bad manners to lick our plates clean as long as it was done quietly. No use either the cat looking hopefully on, there would be nothing left for her, she had to catch her own.

At Saturday tea time a small tin of sardines or corned beef was shared between us and Our Dad always made a point of encouraging us to eat lots of bread with it. Normally amongst members of our family there was continuous hubbub of chatter, playful banter and squabbles. But when we visited grandparents and especially at meal times we were perfectly silent.

Dad, "All on y' 'a' got a nice piece o' bully biff so spin it out an' yut yups o' bread wi'it. An' dussunt lean back on thic there chair, dald thee eyes, I've told thee afore about that."

15

As with all children, there were various foods we disliked, but there was no point in voicing our disapproval to Our Dad, however contritely. It was useless bellyaching that the meat was too fatty for instance, even if it was all fat. With a slight hint of irritation, concealing considerable annoyance, Our Dad would retaliate, "It's fattier where there's none, you'll yut it all up an' like it."

Sunday dinner was the meal of the week, a veritable feast, with perhaps a drop of cider, and afters too. We were reminded of those who had little to eat and instructed to leave nothing. Quite often Our Pug would stubbornly refuse to eat his, often watching it get more and more unpalatable until tea time. If he was lucky he would be rescued, when, without Our Dad knowing, Our Ger sneaked in to bolt it down for him.

Dad, "It's no good thee grizzlin' about it, make no mistake thee'st got t' yut thee vittles. I d' wanna see thy plate clane when I d' come back in a vyow minutes. An' when thee'st cleared that cabbage up thee'st gotta gollop that rice puddin' down, ... all on't."

Water for Drinking and Washing

If y' got t' carry yer own wayter y' byunt extravagant wi' it.

It was to be many years before the mains water supply was brought to our home. However, all the cottages in the district had a well in the garden to supply water for drinking and cooking purposes. Our Dad regularly warned us to keep away from ours and fitted it with a large heavy lid. One glimpse into the black hole was enough to satisfy our natural curiosity, convincing us that it really was dangerous. The water we drew was wonderfully thirst-quenching and so deliciously cool, even in the hottest weather.

The well was useful during sultry summers in another way too; we often lowered meat, milk and margarine into its chilly depths to prevent the hot weather from causing it to 'go off'.

Sometimes though, following a prolonged dry spell. the water level would fall so low we would have to use another source.

Ger, "Kip back a bit more Our Ov, in case theze 'ere 'andle d' fly round a bit quick."

There were a number of shallow wells in the area. The setting of one we knew as 'Granny's Well' was delightful. It was in a small cutting near the top of a hill and from it, over fields full of lark song, one enjoyed a panoramic view of the Severn Vale and distant Cotswolds. Overhung with catkins, the magic dell was bedecked with primroses, bluebells, violets, windflowers and later in the year spotted orchids and scented wild thyme. It could only have raised one's spirits to have drawn water in this enchanting place, but now it is hidden beneath brambles.

The picture shows Our Dad collecting water from the shallow well that we used when the one in our garden dried up. It was a very old and reliable spring at the bottom of a steep sided valley and must have been used and maintained for generations by local cottagers.

Dad, "There's a frog in 'ere, d' y' reckon we ought t' leave'n, ar 'ould ern o' y' like 'n in a cup o' wayter?"

Many years ago the spring had been enclosed with stonework, and other large slabs of stone formed a simple roof. Now, the inside was covered with mosses and ferns. We watched as Our Dad dipped the buckets in turn into the clear, cool water, carefully avoiding the the pond skaters, water boatmen and the frog that sometimes lived there. He took the brimming buckets separately up the steep slippery bank to a nearby track, then hitched them to his yoke. He carried them almost half a mile home, any slight stumble causing the water to slop out, resulting not only in wet legs, but an earlier return journey.

Some of us children accompanied Our Dad and, during the outward trip, we set aside armloads of wood which we always collected later. It wouldn't do to return empty-handed.

Dad, "We left thic burden o' 'ood in the vyarn here somewhere, cun y' remember where 'twas?"

Water was also needed for laundering clothes. For this and other purposes rainwater was channelled through guttering and drainpipes from the roof of our cottage and sheds into water butts and our big red cylindrical tank.

It must have been hard work using the dolly tub and turning the handle of the mangle. Our Den and Our Thynt did a lot of washing and ironing but a kindly neighbour did most of it. Something that reduced the work further for us was the fact that at night we boys slept in the same shirts that we had worn all day. We had heard that posh people wore pyjamas, but that would have required extra laundering; we considered them sissyish anyhow and I think we would have rioted had we been asked to wear underpants.

Den, "Watch out then, mind yer fingers."

When the wicker basket was overflowing with dirty clothes, we sat it precariously on top of a wheelbarrow or our small trolley to take it to Mrs. Cooper. She did most of the washing and ironing for us.

In those days clothes were laundered because they were dirty; the smell of sweat under the arms of a shirt would certainly not justify washing it. But the job was exhausting. the fire beneath the copper had to be lit before breakfast and after considerable effort, beating the washing in the dolly tub and scrubbing with block soap, the clothes would still have to be rinsed, put through the mangle and dried before they could be ironed.The dank, musty smell of steamy wet washing that hung about Mrs. Cooper's back kitchen remains even more unforgettable than the neatly folded spring-fresh laundry we collected in the trolley later.

Thynt, "Mind them bumps Our Al ar we'll 'a' this lot over."

The big round water tank had been repaired in many places and regularly sprung leaks. Our Dad felt that it was near the end of its useful life and not really large enough to store sufficient water for the needs of our growing family. His solution was to build a reservoir, a project which occupied us all for some time. The bigger boys were set to work digging and carting soil and concrete, while we smaller children looked for stones which we smashed into chips to mix in with the concrete. The walls and top of the reservoir were reinforced with old iron bedsteads that we found in quarries. The reservoir was eventually finished and held about six hundred gallons of water. It gave good service for over forty years before it was broken up.

Dad, "If y' d' goo an' get me a piece o' black lead, I'll try an' work out how much more cement we got t' get t' make anough concrete fer the top."

Our Al is having his hair cut. Our Mame's and mine have been done. Our Dad's next job will be to sharpen a saw for a neighbour; he normally did this outside as it required good light. Behind him, next to the reservoir, is a pile of riddled ashes to burn on the back kitchen stove.

Beyond the reservoir is the big red water tank. Sometimes, when the level in the tank was very low, we tipped it over, cleaned the sludge out and painted it inside and out with red oxide paint. Our big red tank was like an old friend. As children we bumped it hard to listen to the satisfying booming sound as it shuddered, and tapped it lightly to judge the amount of water inside. We loved the peculiar muffled echoes as we shouted into the tank when the water level was low. When the tank was full we sailed boats, but the thing we enjoyed most was to poke a finger ever so gently at the mosquito larvae as they hung suspended from the water surface to watch them wriggle down into the depths then float slowly back to the top again.

Dad, "Give I a shout if I d' cut thee ear off ootn't?"

Our Pug could be really awkward and stubborn. Here he is insisting that he was first to be ready for his morning wash. Our Den and Our Ger, being bigger, would often provoke him artfully, making sure he didn't get his own way, even if sometimes it caused them some discomfort.

Our Dad buried a pipe from the reservoir under the stone path to a pump in the back kitchen. A few strokes to and fro on the handle brought water gushing into the bowl. Water for drinking and cooking still had to be carried of course, but the addition of the reservoir and pump meant that, for many purposes, we now had an inside water supply - a real luxury. We had always been very economical with the use of this precious commodity; one bowl of cold water had to be sufficient to wash five or six faces clean. Our Dad made a soakaway for used water but it could only cope with small amounts so we generally threw the dirty water across the garden as we always had.

Pug, "Thee'st needn't gyule, thee duss knaw I was vust."

On Friday nights the tin bath was taken from its hook outside the back kitchen and a few inches of warm water put in. The complicated procedure then began. First we younger children stripped off to the waist, knelt in turn at the side of the bath, and washed 'down as far as possible'. We dried and put clean shirts on (that felt good). Then, with the water becoming colder and colder, and still wearing our shirts, we took turns to stand in the bath and wash 'up as far as possible'. A bit of old sacking kept our feet off the cold floor when we dried. When we younger children were in bed the older members of the family repeated the ritual. The single small towel by now was pretty wet!

The gloomy candlelight reflecting off the rough, whitewashed walls, hardly made the blackout at the windows necessary, though it was enough to bath by.

Notice our old black stove, the copper in the corner and a box of kindling wood ready for the morning.

Ger, "Hurry up an' wesh thee vit, that wayter ull be freezin'."

Sundays

No you cawnt cos it be Sunday.

Potatoes formed by far the largest part of any cooked meal we ate. On Sunday mornings all of us boys sat down together to peel them for dinner, our midday meal. Our Thynt and Our Dad would be busy in the back kitchen preparing other vegetables and fruit so there wasn't enough room for us. If it was raining we did the job in the shed but normally we worked outside. It was necessary to fill two saucepans and to ensure we didn't peel too thickly we were told repeatedly, "The best part of taters be next to the skin." We co-operated well with this task because, when it was completed, we had to get out of the way, so before attending Sunday School, we would go for a long walk, birds'-nesting or chasing rabbits.

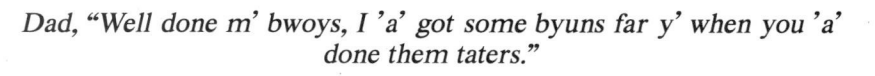

Dad, "Well done m' bwoys, I 'a' got some byuns far y' when you 'a' done them taters."

The way our family spent Sundays conformed closely to rigid puritanical ideas, accepted widely at the time, and fully endorsed in our case, by Our Dad and Grancher Kear. We had to attend chapel two or three times and anything resembling pleasure was strictly forbidden. After helping to prepare vegetables for our midday meal we did no more work, neither were we allowed to play. We were constantly reminded that Sunday was a day of rest. But the reality didn't always match the ideal and we were able to find vacant moments for enjoyment. Silence was imperative though, a bouncing ball, the swish of a skipping rope, or even a raised voice and Our Dad's heavy tread would be heard. The result was a severe telling off. Reading comics was not approved of either, but at least we could do it quietly and no-one need know.

Ger, "Stop wurrutin' you two, Our Dad wun' know cos him's 'avin'
a nap under the apple trees."

The most evocative sound of a lazy hot Sunday afternoon was the persistent cackling of a hen announcing that she had laid another egg. It was almost the only sound heard too, even when as a diversion from the harsh regime we raced caterpillars.

We found them better than snails, they looked more purposeful and were faster too. Not many weeds gained a foothold in our garden but during summer we could always find a good supply of cinnabar caterpillars on some groundsel. We each chose a favourite, lined them up, and with voices rarely raised above a whisper, urged them to sprint across the stone slabs of the path. If Our Dad came by we quickly covered them up or pretended we hadn't noticed them. To a Methodist of the time this innocent childhood amusement would be seen as the first downward step to a life of gambling and profligacy at the racecourse.

Pug, "Mine's gwain t' win agyun cos nern o' yours be gwain the right woy."

Our Dad had hung a swing from the damson tree in the Patch. We used it more on Sunday afternoons than at any other time, and being some distance from the cottage it didn't disturb the peace of the day. It was a great source of pleasure for us children but usually several of us would want to use it at the same time. We therefore had to be sensible and take turns or become involved in a noisy squabble which might attract Our Dad's attention, with the result that none of us would be allowed to use it. If, however, one could get the swing to oneself, it was delightful on a hot summer's day to spend a leisurely afternoon swinging dreamily in the deep, cooling shade of the damson tree.

Mame, "I was on these 'ere swing vust, an' I be gwain t' stay 'ere all the a'ternoon. I 'yun' gwain t' move fer nobody."

31

While Our Dad dozed quietly in his chair, or under an apple tree, we boys could only dream of going for a bowler run, playing a ball game or constructing something in the shed.

Our Ov and Mame were permitted more freedom perhaps; that was how it seemed to me at any rate and more than once the issue became the subject of an unpleasant arguement. The girls were not allowed to play hopscotch or skip, but even if they did break the rules, they appeared to be treated more leniently than us boys. Sunday didn't seem to affect them so much, but gave them the opportunity to amuse themselves for long periods with their dolls. In a quiet corner they would engage in the usual games that girls do with dolls, recreating and playing through a variety of situations while developing their motherly instincts.

Mame, "My dolly's gwain t' 'ave 'er 'air done then 'ers gwain t' the Co-op."

Quite often on Sunday evenings during the summer, after the last chapel service, we called on Grancher and Granny Childs. This provided an occasion for the girls to deck themselves in their best dresses and ribbons, and Our Thynt could dispense with her boots in favour of shoes. Maybe too, they would be fussed and cuddled a little and told, "My word, you do look pretty."

Our Thynt has been given a few sweets to share out and is offering one each to Our Ov and Mame. Such treats came our way very rarely, no more than once or twice a year, and would be saved until Sunday, the most auspicious day of the week. Then, with due ceremony, they would be shared with scrupulous fairness, we thinking ourselves the luckiest children in the whole world.

Thynt, "Shut yer eyes an' open yer 'ands an' see what God d' send y'
...... Now if y' doan do it nern o' y' ull get one."

33

If the weather was good the whole family went for a walk though the woods or fields before eventually arriving at our grandparents' home. This was a part of Sunday we enjoyed. Nevertheless, in keeping with the spirit of the Sabbath, it was a leisurely activity; more of a contemplative stroll than a walk. No birds'-nesting was allowed, or climbing trees; no splashing in water or tossing a ball to each other. Normally, skipping would not be tolerated either, but my sisters seemed to be able to flaunt rules with greater ease than us boys. Our Dad was probably asking himself if he should put a stop to their enjoyment. I am sure he would if they made too much noise but in the meantime no one could see them. In any case he was probably infringing the sanctity of the holy day himself for he would be mentally noting where firewood and dung could be found in order to send us out for it on Monday.

Dad, "I doan wan' y' brevettin' about a'ter birds' nests t'day, you 'a' got all the wik t' do that."

The severity that characterised Sundays continued when we went to chapel for the evening service. We had to sit very still, and to discourage fidgetting, were made to sit on our hands. In absolute silence, hardly daring to breathe, we listened while the visiting preacher delivered his 'message from God'. Sometimes his tone was gentle, his words persuasive and their meaning plausible. Often though, the preacher harangued us at length, not with the force of religious principle or argument but with what appeared to be personal incontrovertible knowledge gained, apparently, by intimate acquaintance with the the workings of The Almighty's mind - and it was made abundantly clear that if we did not mend our evil ways we faced only everlasting torment.

But I think we knew in our hearts that the rhetoric we so often endured should not be taken too seriously. Local preachers were well- meaning men and women. It was simply something we suffered while dreaming of the pleasanter world waiting for us outside.

Preacher, "An' a . . . ll evil- doers, an' a . . . ll sinners, an' a . . . ll them who 'ave transgressed His 'oly laws ull be rejected an' cast into the everlasting fires of Hell . . . if . . . you doan go to the Lard with a contrite 'eart an' receive His merciful forgiveness . . . t'night."

Only when winter was at its very worst did we use the front room and then only on Sunday evenings. Besides our best furniture it contained the piano. There could be no excuses not to practise now.

The room was small, with little space to move about, but Our Dad had obtained a set of Arthur Mee's Children's Encyclopedia to keep us quiet and on Sundays we were allowed to look at the volumes. Because they were considered precious, he first checked that our hands were clean, then demonstrated how we must turn each page from the top and made certain we supported one side of the book to reduce the strain on its spine. Other large books were popular also, particularly a huge tome we won in a competition at school for killing most cabbage white butterflies.

Thynt, "Come on Our Pug you 'a' lost the place agyun ain y'?"

Messing About in the Woods

God provided trees so we 'ould 'ave summat t' climb.

Just outside our cottage gate were the wide open greens and tumps where we played football, cricket and chasing. Beyond, the vast green playground of the forest beckoned and we took advantage of every opportunity to answer the call. As long as our allotted jobs had been' done, we could enjoy the freedom of the woods, roaming and playing happily, until tired we went home at bedtime. We knew the dangers of climbing and of the abandoned mines, but otherwise there seemed to be nothing that could harm us. Even as we ran unwillingly through the forest to school there might just be time to stop for a moment where the men had been cutting timber. We would clamber over the wood stacks, balance on the prepared trunks or enjoy a swing before, sadly, the sound of the bell put a stop to our fun and we would tear breathlessly into school.

Thynt, "I byunt gwain t' swing y' agyun cos Gunner Kerwood wun'
'alf tell y' off if y' be late fer school."

Children seem to find it essential to behave in an unruly manner when dismissed at the end of a school day. Squirming bottoms are, after spending hours polishing benches, at the command, 'class dismiss', lifted hastily. Stiff limbs are unfolded and voices, which had been under some degree of control, tested.

On our release we pushed through the door, dashed for the gate and raced boisterously to liberty. On our route home, at the edge of the wood, were some smallish trees. They were easy to climb and to celebrate our deliverance we regularly scrambled up one of them, shouting loudly all the time. Once as near the top as we dared venture, we yelled and bawled defiantly at the tops of our voices, turning to face each direction in turn, like animals reinforcing their claim to the territory - after all it was ours.

'Oopin an' 'ollerin' from the tree tops.

39

There was plenty for us to do in 'our' forest. In summer, when the ferns grew tall along the forest rides, we loved to run full pelt and jump into them, relying on the dense growth to cushion our landings. Sometimes we would wriggle on our bellies for some distance between the bracken stems to lie perfectly still and quiet for a few moments, completely hidden from the entire world.

Many birch trees also lined the forest rides; this is how we used to swing them. First we chose a fairly young tree and climbed to the top. (This became increasingly difficult as we got higher, for the tree would sway precariously). Then, while maintaining a firm grip with both hands as high as possible, we kicked our feet outwards into space. The experience was breathtaking. Twigs would brush our faces as we started to fall, quickly at first, then, after five or six feet the natural springiness of the branches, then main trunk, gradually began to take effect and lower us gently to the ground.

Although some trees remained bowed for a day or two, they soon righted themselves, but before we swung a birch tree we made absolutely certain there were no Forestry officers within sight.

"*Whee . . . .*"

Where Blackpool Brook gurgled and splashed through steeper banks, alder trees enclosed it, shutting out much of the light. Many 'ropes' of traveller's joy dangled from the tree tops. Now we knew a little about Tarzan, indeed we had seen him once at the pictures when a kind aunt took us. It would be terrific to swing on creepers just like him. We tested one of the large old stems that had become detached near the ground. Slowly becoming more confident, we swung over the brook, gradually increasing the distance. Eventually, when we were certain it was completely safe, we took turns swinging from the top of the bank high over the water into the upper branches of the trees on the other side yelling all the time like Tarzan. Over a period of time we had enormous fun on our Tarzan swing until it was discovered and broken by other boys.

Den, "There goes Tarzan. Owd on tight an' dussent look down."

We used to cut short-stemmed bracken at the edge of the Aisne to use instead of straw for singeing the hair off the pig's carcass when it had been slaughtered. When the bracken had dried, Our Dad would send us to fetch it, but we were easily sidetracked and might leave the loads temporarily, if something attracted our attention.

Here we are building a stank (dam) at the outlet of a small pond near home. We used sticks, stones and mud to block the flow of water, working hard to stem even the tiniest trickle. When at last the pond was full, it was wonderful fun to breach the dam and follow the onrush of water down through the wood.

Our Den is attending to the wheel of the trolley (we had a lot of trouble with it coming off on rough ground).

Notice also, a 'ship badger' in the background, going to check his sheep.

Den, "Dussent thee cry ow' butt, we ull soon putt theze 'ere wheel back on your pram, 'twunt come off agyun."

We worked and played together as a family a great deal, nevertheless our friends were very important too.

This is the gang to which Our Al and I belonged. Besides playing football and cricket, we went birds'-nesting and climbing and did many other exciting things together. After meeting though, the same question always arose, "What sh' we do?" However, following a long and noisy argument we usually came to a fairly friendly agreement.

During the summer holidays we became Red Indians. Our camp was hidden in the middle of a plantation of young fir trees and approached by a devious route designed to baffle any enemy. We thought our stalking and tracking skills would have rivalled that of any Blackfoot or Mohawk warrior. We used a complicated set of bird calls as signals and were well-armed with quarterstaves, spears and catapults as well as bows and arrows, so we felt totally secure. Any enemy must have been thankful that we never had to use our weapons in anger against them!

A friend, "We ought t' putt some 'eavy tuffuts on top o' our camp in case the wind d' blow 'n down 'sknaw."

The gang is about to explore the entrance to one of the old abandoned pits in the wood near our home. Most of them had been deliberately blocked or were obstructed with piles of household and garden rubbish, With bows of yew wood, like genuine medieval English archers, and spears made of fern stems, our intrepid band approached the gaping holes that would have scared either of us had we been alone.

One of these mines was particularly frightening. In a forgotten spot, on a densely wooded hillside, it could only be reached through a deep cutting. The opening was not blocked but shrouded in brambles and the pit itself was full of water. The echoes of the continuous drip, drip, drip, from the roof were amplified menacingly by the black interior of the cavern. It would have made a perfect lair for some form of ghoulish monster or latter day Grendle.

*A friend, "I d'aim there be a fox ar summat in thic there 'ole.
Theesknaw we ought t' 'ave our weapons ready in case 'im d' jump
out at us."*

44

This is the gang experiencing the breathtaking joys of smoking.

There was no chance of our gang obtaining cigarettes of course, but occasionally we managed to pinch a few matches. We tried smoking all sorts of dry plant stems but found nettle stalks best, putting a lighted match to one end and sucking hard at the other. We hollowed large acorns too and put hollow stems into their sides. On the way to and from school we searched for discarded cigarette ends at the sides of the road and stuffed the remaining tobacco into the pipes, or else we smoked dried leaves. Of course smoking was something our gang did strictly in secret. Our Dad would have seen it as an introduction to an unhealthy and expensive vice.

A friend, "This is the proper woy t' ketch olt of a fag see, cos Our Dad d' smoke an' 'im d' knaw."

It was fun to dig a hole in a bank and create a fireplace, complete with chimney. While keeping a watchful eye open for P.C. Fardon the local bobby, we would light a fire and boil gooseberries or blacken chestnuts or taters, in a vain attempt to roast them. After pretending that the results of our cooking were good, we entertained ourselves in other ways. We might pour a little water into bottles we found, screw the tops on tightly, then throw them on the fire and hide behind a nearby tree to await the explosions. Being aware of the dangers of fire we always made certain it was out, before we left, by peeing on it. At the same time there was no point pilfering matches unless we maximised their use, so when it was getting dark, we set the gorse at the edge of the wood ablaze. As we watched the the flames rushing and crackling through the bushes, brightening the area around, we earnestly hoped that neither P.C. Fardon nor Our Dad had seen us.

A friend, "We ull set the gaust alight a'ter we 'a' douted theze vire an i's darker."

Most small boys must have done this at sometime. The gang is enjoying a simple diversion while on the way home from school. There was little traffic on the road in those days so not much chance of anyone's contribution being cut short. The aim was to produce a longer stream than the previous day. At playtimes, we small boys would strive to see who could make the highest mark on the urinal wall. On a good day, one boy, the envy of the lower juniors, could manage to clear it. He enjoyed much admiration amongst us but only the dunces would stand close to the champion.

The box at the roadside contains a gas mask. The jars are full of a mixture of drinking chocolate and sugar, which together with items of clothing, were supplied by America to help us through the war.

A freind, "T'morra we ull all ex Miss if her ull let us 'ave an extra bottle of milk each."

Our Ov and Mame played houses on the green with their friends. Once the size and shape of the house had been agreed, and outlined with small stones, they decorated each room with bits and pieces they found in quarries and on ash tips. Broken china served as ornaments, old tins and jars as cups and pots. They smeared lots of blackberry juice, if any was available, on their mouths as lipstick, and with exaggerated mannerisms and suitably affected voices, acted the parts of various female characters. They pretended their husbands were working at the pit and would soon be home for tea. Mud pies would have to be made and decorated, and flowers arranged. Some roles, of course, called for a more authoritative interpretation than others, which gave some of them a chance to show off and impress their friends.

Mame, "You shouldn't 'a' put them stones there Our Ov. Now remember you be my little girl an' y' gotta do as I d' say goo on out t' play ull y'?"

Family Walks

The easiest woy droo the 'ood is t' volla the path.

Our Dad rode his motorbike to and from the factory where he worked. On his way home he always knocked it out of gear and switched the engine off to freewheel down the slope of Cut 'n Fry Green to our cottage. Some Saturdays in spring and summer, if he had no other commitments and the weather was good, he would promise us a long walk with perhaps a picnic in the afternoon, as long as we completed certain jobs he set during the the morning. Just before he was due home at dinner time, feeling confident our tasks had been done to the standard he required, we ran excitedly to meet him at the top of Cut 'n Fry Green. Eventually, when he arrived, we clambered on to his bike for a ride home, anticipating a wonderful afternoon.

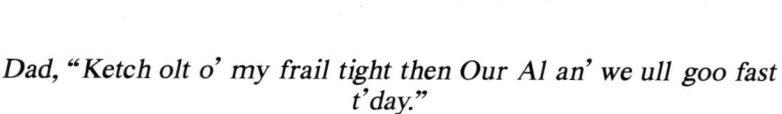

Dad, "Ketch olt o' my frail tight then Our Al an' we ull goo fast t'day."

We often walked to Blackpool Brook. It was not far so we usually took some of the boats we had made. Despite the fact that the cold water made our feet ache we spent many happy hours playing. Apart from sailing boats there were pretty pebbles to find, squelchy red clay to shape and if we were lucky a few small trout to trap. We younger children were fascinated by the semi-hard tablets of smooth clay material in the water, we knew it as 'gypsy soap'. It felt and functioned like soap but was more pleasant to use than carbolic. The older children spent much of their time 'stanking' the stream only to thrill at the sight of the water rushing out when they broke the dam down. At last, when the evening air began to cool, we dried our feet and legs and made our way home, tired out but happy.

Yet, before we stepped out of the woods into Cut 'n Fry Green, Our Dad would expect each of us to be carrying an armload of firewood to toss on to the woodpile.

Al, "Im's a sailin' out o' the 'arbour a long woy across the sea to a voreign country t' fetch a yup o' bananas fer us."

Excitement was at its highest if, on a Saturday, Our Dad announced that we would walk to the River Severn. We might go to Gatcombe, Milkamead or Severn Bridge. If we took a jar of earthworms we could catch flatfish or eels for Sunday breakfast. We could paddle in the muddy rock pools , or simply watch the water, the trains, the salmon fishermen with their lave nets on the sand bars or the hundreds of house martins that nested under the stone arches of the bridge. We usually had a picnic tea and then, as the evening approached, sounds seemed to carry more clearly. We listened to the martins as they swooped and wheeled for flies. We might even hear the sea cadets on the training ship Vindicatrix at evening muster, over a mile away across the water. But sooner or later all sounds were drowned and the attention seized by the muffled roar and the awesome sight of the all-devouring Severn tide as it rushed up the narrowing estuary, quickly swallowing the rocks we had just been playing on.

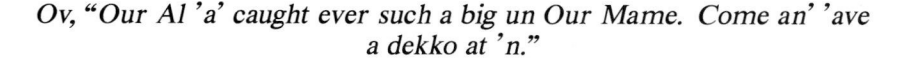

Ov, "Our Al 'a' caught ever such a big un Our Mame. Come an' 'ave a dekko at 'n."

Here we are making our way home from the Severn. Our Den is carrying a light canvas sheet. We took it when the weather looked unsettled to shelter beneath if a storm broke.

For much of the journey we wandered here and there searching for birds' nests and rabbits, or we stopped to explore a brook for trout and bullheads. We liked to climb on the wooden railings of a fence too, to watch the soldiers at the searchlight station at the top of the hill.

The girls couldn't resist gathering a few flowers to decorate our cottage. They picked them with urgency to avoid being left behind, then ran ahead again to find more.

The journey was long and mostly uphill, so eventually we younger children grew tired. Our Dad sometimes found it necessary to give Our Ov and Mame a piggyback for much of the way. Indeed, had it been a year earlier, one of them would have been carried on his shoulders while the other would have been enjoying a ride in a back pack he had made.

Dad, "Mind where y' be a drowin' them there doin's you bwoys ar you'll 'a' somebody's eye on th' end. An' you girls, doan gether too many o' them, cos them d' look prettier where um be."

Sometimes, on Bank Holidays, Aunty Alice managed to persuade Uncle Ted to borrow a donkey for the day and, together with some of our cousins, we scrambled aboard the tiny cart to go to Milkamead. Uncle Ted led the procession at donkey's pace while at the rear three or four of our aunts spread themselves across the road earnestly exchanging gossip. Uncle Ted always seemed to be in a crabby mood on these occasions. He knew the ladies would want a cup of tea when we at last reached the Severn, and he would have to light a fire and find some clean water. No doubt too, he was peeved by the fact that Our Dad had wangled a day off.

When eventually we reached our destination, the donkey was tethered beneath some trees at the end of a lane while we walked through the field to the river.

Once the donkey freed herself while we were picnicking and found her own way home drawing an empty cart. With tempers sorely frayed we were left with no choice but to walk the three miles back home.

Uncle Ted, "Come on y' sodding mokey, shift thee gurt hommocks oot, thouse got a long woy t' goo y't."

There were many small free mines in the Forest, each operated by one or two men keen to be their own bosses. We liked to look around them, at the apparatus and into the dark mine entrances. We shuddered as Our Dad asked, "How would you like to work down there with just a candle for light?"

Although some mines were more elaborate than others, the sites usually looked chaotic, as if everything had been constructed hurriedly overnight, then deserted suddenly. There appeared to be no concessions to efficient coal production. Nevertheless, the gale holders exercised a lot of practical ingenuity, much of their apparatus being fabricated from rejected articles and junk. On one site, an old car had been tied to a tree and its back axle supported on stones with the winch cable running around a tyreless rear wheel. Not only was the old car used to haul drams out of the mine in this way, but also served as a store shed, there being no building on the site.

Al, "The mon who d' turn thic 'andle ull have the same amount o' work t' do so I cawnt see how the little cog cun make it easier."

Our favourite walks were through areas of coppiced woodland, especially in spring when the ground was carpeted with bluebells, primroses, celandines and anemones. This was the best sort of place to exercise our birds'-nesting skills too.

We found fir plantations relatively dead, yet the peculiar resinous smell, the murmuring as the wind worked among the tree tops and the darkness beneath, held a fascination of their own.

The charcoal burner in the background of the picture is attending his portable kilns. He preferred to use hardwoods, relying on a supply of fairly small pieces up to four or five inches thick. His shelter is nearby, for he watched his kilns both day and night.

Where mature stands of trees had been clear-felled, stately foxgloves soon moved in to heal the scars. We were very fond of foxgloves and used their trumpets as finger puppets or else we popped them like balloons. We knew them as snompers. Bird's-foot trefoil was eggs and bacon, white horehound was bobbies' buttons and lady's smock, because of its affinity for wet ground, was known as pee the beds.

Mame, "I sh' be glad when we be wum so I cun coochy down an' goo t' sleep cos my legs d' ache like billyo".

This is the Dilley, an American army rubbish tip. During the war, at a time of material shortage, it was felt that American soldiers enjoyed relative luxury, so many local people walked to the dump in search of articles that could possibly have some use. Stories abounded of the marvellous items found, but we were happy to come away with shiny buttons, badges, knives and sometimes American comics and magazines, though Our Dad didn't approve of these. The treasures were proudly shown off to our friends and the usual swopping took place. There were also practical things to be found, an odd tool, bits of pipe and metal, and lengths of wood and boxes. Like magpies, we took everything we could if we thought it might come in useful one day.

If, on our walks to or from the Dilley, we saw American army trucks drive by, we yelled out as loudly as we could, "Any gum chum?". Occasionally we were lucky and the soldiers would toss out a packet of biscuits or chewing gum to us.

Al, "I d' reckon it be off an American airplane".

We always looked forward eagerly to our Saturday evening walk but sometime in September, as summer gave way to autumn, Our Dad would say, "If we d' take a jam jar along we might see a feow blackberries." We knew this low-key approach meant that instead of the usual walk, we would all be going out to pick as many blackberries as we could before it got dark. Our Dad knew very well where they were to be found and over the following weekends we gathered a number of baskets full. He never missed an opportunity of adjusting the circumstances of our walk if it could be made profitable.

At first we resented the fact that we would miss the enjoyment of our usual ramble, but after overcoming our initial reluctance, blackberrying gave us enormous pleasure and satisfaction in spite of thorns, scratches and perhaps a wasp sting. Besides, the fruit was free and together with apples made the most delicious jam.

Ger, "There be yups round ' ere, you cawnt 'elp bumping into um."

58

Sheep's Snouts, Foxwhelps and Cider

Apples be good, whether raw, cooked or gently fermented as cider.

We delighted in picking apples from the trees in the Patch. It was far easier to achieve visible results than when blackberrying, and the delicious smell of the fruit added to our joy. We liked scrambling around in the trees to reach the more inaccessible fruit, but perhaps tended to show off a little. Our Dad knew that his presence reduced the chances of an accident as we were less inclined to horse around with him on the scene.

The apples were stored in the top shed and, in fruitful years, under our beds as well. Our Dad continually impressed upon us the importance of not bruising the fruit, but any that were damaged were set aside for immediate use or piled with the windfalls ready for cider-making.

Den, "Come on then Walley 'ammond, see if thee const ketch theze un."

Mr. Markey had a cider mill. He also had a lot of apple trees, so allowed us to top up our supply of fruit from his orchard.

On the evening earmarked for cider-making, we children ate our tea early to take advantage of the diminishing daylight, and taking some empty sacks, dragged the trolley of windfalls to Mr. Markey's orchard to pick up more. As soon as Our Dad had bolted his evening meal he joined us. It didn't matter what varieties we used but quantity was important. Kingston Blacks, Dymock reds, Foxwhelps and Sheep's Snouts were tossed into the sacks. Tom Putt kept company with Granny Smith and Lane's Prince Albert joined Early Victoria. We threw in pears too and sprays of elderberries, and beetroot to give the cider more colour. Sometimes wasps were troublesome, and one or two of us might be stung, but with bulging sacks neatly stacked outside the mill, we waited in eager anticipation for Mr. Markey to begin the process.

Dad. "We 'a' got t' get a muv on mind. Mr. Markey ull be ready t' putt um droo the mill d' rectly, doan matter if a vyow daddecky uns d' goo in the bags."

61

While Our Dad and my bigger brothers undertook the strenuous job of keeping the wheels of the mill turning steadily, Our Al and I poured apples into the box at the top of the crusher. We watched as they dropped between two heavy spiked rollers, where they were mashed to a course pulp. Mr. Markey used a wooden box with a handle attached as a large shovel to throw the crushed apples to one side. When all the fruit had been put through the mill once, Mr. Markey adjusted the rollers with a big spanner to bring them much closer together. On feeding the fruit through the mill a second time the apples were reduced to a soft aromatic juicy mush ready for the press.

Mr. Markey was a tough, wiry man who moved rapidly and stopped suddenly like a weasel. We loved to see him in action but wondered how he could manage to talk as much as he did without the thin roll-up cigarette falling from his lips.

Mr. Markey, "I should 'elp youer feyther wi' them bags out there if I was you, cos if I d' pick y' up in theze 'ere shovel I might drop y' in thic crusher.......accidental like."

In the failing light, Mr. Markey, fag still hanging miraculously from his bottom lip has filled another mat with pulp and is levelling it before folding the corners down tidily. The wooden frame helps him to keep the cheese neat and vertical. It is held in place by a couple of long wire rods. These will be withdrawn in order to raise the frame, then replaced to support it in a higher position for the next mat. As the layers of the cheese are formed, we look for the very first drop of juice and watch excitedly as it trickles with increasing speed in the channel of the stone slab before dropping into the well.

With the build up of more tiers, the edges of the bulging mats begin to glisten with sweet liquid and the slow drip, drip, drip, increases steadily as the liquor begins to run freely.

Mr. Markey, *"Well, if 'tyunt no good when we 'a' finished ow' butty, thee const always tell thee feyther him cun wesh 'is vit in it ar dab it behind 'is ears."*

The scene is now brightened a little by Mr. Markey's carbide lamp.

The cheese has been constructed and boards and blocks positioned to ensure an even distribution of pressure. At each addition of weight the liquid pours a little faster. Mr. Markey pushes a bar through the slot in the end of the large screw until it meets the blocks below. As the cheese is compressed the flow immediately becomes a flood and the well begins to fill. A bucket is held underneath, a barrel rolled into position and we begin to fill it. When Mr. Markey has offered his opinion on the probable quality of the resulting cider, it will be time for us to dip the scoop into the flow for a taste. But first we are given grim warnings of the devastating effects of sampling too much - it is likely to send us running for the nearest bushes with our trousers down.

Mr. Markey, "Hey Zurree, this ull kip thee in at nights.. I'll warrant thouse got a drop o' good stuff 'ere owld un."

I am sure Our Dad enjoyed pouring the sweet fluid into the barrels. But he was rather concerned too, for if there was insufficient to top up the casks to the brim, water would have to be added - a course to be avoided if at all possible.

As the stream of juice from the cheese diminished, Our Dad and Mr. Markey pushed a longer bar into the slot to get more leverage. The screw was turned and little by little the cheese was compressed further and the flow restored. It was left under pressure overnight in an effort to extract every last drop of liquor.

When the first cask was full, and we had cleared up, we set it carefully on the big trolley and cushioned it with sacks. Cold and tired, but very happy, we pushed our cargo home. Of course, on this occasion, Our Dad ensured that we took especial care to steer clear of any bumps and ruts.

Mr. Markey, "I daresn't bend about too much ar it d' ketch I in the back 'sknaw......an I'll tell thee it doan 'alf putt I droo the hoops too."

65

The following evening we fetched the second barrel from the mill, after it had been topped up with cider which had drained from the cheese overnight.

Both casks were manoeuvred into position on a specially made frame or a couple of sturdy wooden boxes. However, Our Dad remained anxious until, after a day or two, he heard the hissing and saw the frothing of the early fermentation. Each year he talked of putting pieces of bacon into the barrels, it was supposed to 'feed' the yeast. But I don't think he did it very often. He was not the sort of man to throw into a barrel meat which he would have preferred on his plate, or risk spoiling cider he had laboured so hard to make.

Our Dad was not a drinking man, but after a couple of months, when the fermentaion had stopped, he sampled the results of his work, smacking his lips with obvious relish after every mouthful.

Dad, "A'ter we 'a'wangled 'n droo the gate y' cun 'elp me oik' n up the step an' in t' the shed. It'll be youer bedtime then."

If any of us behaved badly we suffered a good hiding. I dreaded Our Dad's anger. Retribution was swift and neat; there was no escape. Between the time of the first quiverings of my bottom lip and the time when my backside felt as if it was on fire, came a barrage of hard, well-aimed smacks with a big rugged open hand. The action was reinforced with dire warnings and the certain promise that next time I wouldn't be let of so lightly. Floods of tears followed, and lusty howling - it seemed it would never stop. If I protested, I was dragged unceremoniously to the long shed and locked in until I was silent, or until Our Dad remembered me. Here the yelling and bawling went on. Sometimes, in temper, I would kick the door or beat it with a hammer or wooden mallet, but this only invited another leathering.

Dad, "I'll teach thee not t' try an' arg' wi' me, thee see if I don't y' young Isaac. I'll warm thy backside up fer thee, make no mistake, an' if thee dussunt stop 'owlin' an' snivellin' thee const have another dose."

Locked alone in the shed I hid in the darkest corner or under the workbench making myself as tiny as I could; a pitiful little bundle of misery, convulsing vigorously and weeping bitterly. Eventually the tears would dry up, but the uncontrollable breathless sobbing continued.

I wallowed in self-pity but found no comfort as I considered my own wretchedness. No one cared for me; everything in the world seemed more agreeable and kinder than people. Very slowly self-pity gave way to painful self- examination until I began unconsciously to fiddle with something at hand. I might poke a finger in my ear, or tug at the loose wool on my jersey, or worry away at a nail in a piece of timber. At last I would clamber out from my cramped hiding place to nose around silently in what seemed a prison cell. I remember peeping into Our Dad's big wooden tool chest and leaning over the old tub of pig food to allow the meal to run through my fingers. I would search for something to do before being released, and that is how I 'discovered' the cider

" 'Twasn't my fault."

We each made 'the discovery' on different occasions during our childhood, usually as a result of being locked alone in the shed for bad behaviour. Why we made the find in this way I do not know. We knew where the cider casks were; went past them several times each day, but the wonderful implications of this knowledge didn't dawn on us until we had the opportunity for long private meditation that detention in the shed offered. When at last we understood, we enjoyed in full the luxury of refreshment on tap.

First we took the vital precaution of ensuring that Our Dad was nowhere near, then stole quietly into the shed. It was not at all comfortable lying on one's side, mouth wide open beneath the tap, but most agreeable when the delicious liquid dribbled in. Though we were discreet, and didn't overindulge, Our Dad must have been suspicious when we left the shed sometimes, and no doubt guessed why the supply didn't last as long as it ought.

Pug, "I 'ouldn't 'ave too much mind ar it'll give thee the collywobbles, i's my turn t' quat down an' 'ave another drop anyroad."

Too much new cider gave us belly ache, but if either of us had a bad cold we were sometimes given a cup of hot cider at bedtime to help 'sweat it out'. For most illnesses Our Dad gave us a cup of ellum blo' tea (an infusion of dried elder flowers). It tasted pretty awful and one mouthful was enough to make us determined to get better in the shortest possible time.

A bruised or swollen ankle was immersed in Colders, a nearby stream noted for its very cold water. Fifteen minutes or so of the treatment turned the original ache into an acute pain for a time, but it seemed to work.

A few greater celandine plants grew near the well and the bright yellow sap was a certain cure for warts, while a plantain leaf wrapped over a boil or sore at bedtime would draw all the pus out cleanly by the morning.

Sometimes a more serious illness visited our cottage, when a call from the doctor and long and tender nursing by Our Thynt and Our Den was necessary to effect a recovery.

Thynt, "The doctor said if y' d' drink this you ull veel better, so come on my babby 'ave a spoonful then y' cun coochy down an' goo t' sleep agyun."

Winter Evenings

It's never too dark t'do a job that d'need doin'.

During the dark winter evenings our cottage, with its cold stone floors, was decidedly draughty. Wind whistled under all three doors that opened into the living room. The oil lamp too, shed only a gloomy light. We had heard of course, that rich people had electric light, but we were used to the conditions and fully accepted them.

Provided we had no jobs to do outside, and were not making a mat at the moment, we occupied ourselves with reading and board games. We all enjoyed drawing too, but had hardly any paper to work on. The margins of the newspaper were useful, while the occasional used envelope was a coveted prize.

For part of the evening Our Dad, sitting at the other end of the room, perused the columns of the Daily Herald. We knew he would get angry if we got in his light, even for a second, so we crouched low when we crossed the room to avoid casting a shadow on his newspaper. Consequently one of the best places to play was under the table.

Ov, "Ave I got time t' get my dolly an' quatty down under the table t' play fer a bit before bedtime, Thynty?"

Our boots, like our clothes, were handed from the eldest as far down the line to the youngest as they could be made to go. Usually Our Dad mended them at his bench in the shed, but on the coldest winter evenings he did the job by the fire in the kitchen. He used leather from old discarded boots, sometimes found thrown out in quarries, to patch the sides and build up the soles and heels. He finished the job by nailing a set of studs to the soles, with the result that members of our family could easily be singled out as we clumped along the road to school.

Often, while the rest of us children read or drew, Our Thynt and Our Den patched clothes or darned socks. Out Thynt was an expert at knitting socks too, using wool unrun from other garments, though she had difficulty 'turning' the heels.

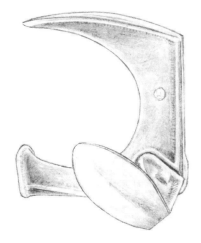

Dad, "Thee bist a bit of a tartar mind. Why duss kip squappin' over on thee vit, dussunt know 'ow to walk ar what?"

On Saturday evenings in winter, we were allowed to stay up late, so we made ourselves snug. The blackout was fitted to the window early, the fire built up and sacks put at the bottom of the draughty doorways. After playing or drawing for a while, we pulled the sofa close to the fire and settled as cosily as possible. Our Dad switched his wireless on; it was his pride and joy. He put his feet up and closed his eyes; rarely was he so relaxed.

He listened to a variety programme and now and again a broad grin spread across his face as a comic turn amused him, but usually it wasn't long before we heard him snoring gently. When Big Ben began to strike nine o'clock, there was a sudden flurry of activity, for inevitably the sound woke Our Dad and the four youngest of us had to be in bed before the clock had finished striking.

Den, "'Ast thou fastened the fowls in an' got the marnin's 'ood, cos i's thy turn t'night mind?"

In the mornings before we left for school, the lavatory was much in demand. If it was occupied by an older brother and I wanted to use it urgently, he would instruct me to run to the bottom of the garden, count to one hundred and then return. He would have left, of course, by the time I ran back. The idea must have prevented a certain amount of embarrassment, while the wait seemed shorter and fraught with a little less desperation. Furthermore, my counting improved - it became much quicker.

At night, images of terrible monsters prowling in the dark shadows of creaking sheds and water tanks haunted us when we needed the lavatory. For a small child it was terrifying. We were, in fact, fortunate if we had the use of a candle, and very lucky indeed to reach the lavatory without it going out. Inside, the draught continued to cause the flame to flicker frighteningly, throwing sinister moving shadows on to walls and floor and we were scared that at any moment it would blow out.

"Please candle doan blow out."

Bedtime for the four youngest of us was at about seven o'clock most evenings. We were supposed to leave our clothes in neat piles on the sofa, but the one large heap that normally resulted could be sorted out in the morning. After undressing, we tore through the front room in complete darkness, and swinging around the knob at the bottom of the banister rail, bolted up the stairs at great speed as if something was chasing us. Only when Mrs. Billington came to our cottage, to give my older brothers piano lessons, did we have the comfort of the dim light that filtered upstairs from the front room.

Mrs. Billington was a fragile, waspish lady, who looked in danger of being blown away by a puff of wind. We children thought her a very odd little woman and found it hard to stifle our giggles whenever we saw her. We referred to her as Mrs. Bee and dared each other to address her as such when we wished her goodnight.

Mame, "Im's playin' that ever s' good t' night en 'im Mrs. Billington?"

76

In our bedroom were two double beds and a chest of drawers; there was room for nothing else. It slept all five of us boys and Our Dad.

At night, during the war, we often heard aeroplanes droning overhead. With the authority only an eldest brother can command, Our Den would pronounce on whether they were British or German. If they were British we could sleep peacefully, but if they were enemy planes I lay very still, almost afraid to breathe until they were out of earshot, convinced Hitler had sent them especially to bomb me. Some winter evenings we watched searchlights probing the skies over the Severn estuary. On many occasions, when Our Den and Ger came to bed, they gazed out of the bedroom window giving accounts of bombs falling amidst incredible dog-fights, with Spitfires and Hurricanes destroying Messerschmitts and Heinkels twenty miles away over Bristol. It was many years before I realised they had made it all up, except for the light from fires, as Bristol was badly bombed at this time.

Ger, "Crimes, them 'yunt 'alf gooin' at it t'night byun' um, it d'give thee the wind up doan it?"

In summertime, from my place in bed, I could gaze out across peaceful fields , and while watching cattle or sheep or a distant tractor I could easily get off to sleep. If, however, I had not dropped off by the time the older boys got to bed, sleep was impossible for a long time.

One or other would start to make up a story, so fantastic as to capture the attention completely.

Outrageous ideas were contributed by any of us who cared to join in. Our efforts, accompanied by chuckles and embarrassed giggles, were as crude as our relatively innocent minds could manage.

Often one of us would begin a silly rhyme,

"Mrs. Powell had a fowl,
    Wrapped 'n in a little
    towel."

At first new verses were added quickly,

"Mr. Haines called 'n funny
    names.
    Ernie Morgan taught 'n t'
    play the organ." etc.

Each new line was followed by uncritical boisterous laughter. But gradually, the time intervals between the ideas lengthened as we grew tired, or a shout from Our Dad at the bottom of the stairs brought an uneasy silence. Eventually, we settled quietly and one by one drifted into sleep.

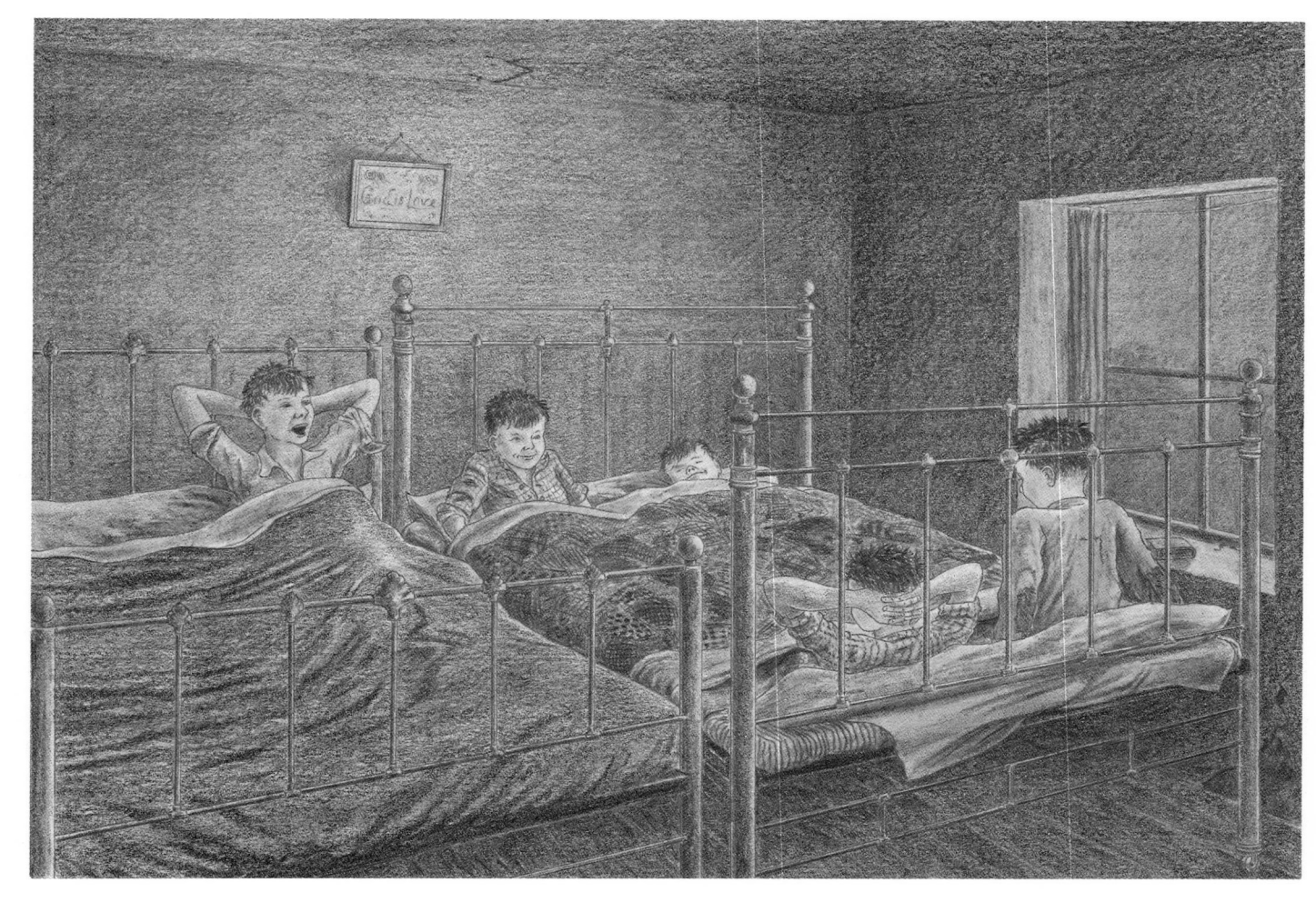

Den, "Which d' wiffle most, Our Pug's breath ar Our Al's vit?"

Glossary

Foresters tend to shorten words a great deal, dropping aitches and omitting word endings. The authentic sound cannot be conveyed entirely faithfully in print, so there must be an element of compromise in written dialect. However, I hope this glossary will be of some help to those not familiar with the Forest of Dean.

agyun	again, against
aim	expect, suppose
ain	haven't
ar	or
bathered out	exhausted, tired
bellock	bellow, shout, cry
bile	boil
billyo	a great deal, quickly
bist	from the verb 'to be'; used with archaic pronouns 'thee' and 'thou'
black lead	graphite or pencil
brevetting	wandering about
browst	twigs
butt or butty	friend
bwoy	boy
byuns	beans
byunt	from the negative form of the verb 'to be'; I byunt, you byunt etc. ('yunt is a shortened form, 'yun' is shortened even more)
byut	beat
cawnt	cannot
clane	clean
clate off	clear off
comp	candle
con	see 'cun'
const	canst, the archaic form of the auxilary verb 'can'
coopies	an infantile word for fowls
cosn't	cannot, used only with archaic pronouns 'thee' and 'thou'
crimes	an expression of astonishment
cun	auxiliary verb, 'can' (sometimes the harder sound 'con' is used)
cooch or coochy	snuggle (a cooch is also a dog kennel)
daaze	euphemistic word for damn
daddecky	partly rotten
daggled	exhausted, tired
dald	euphemistic word for damn
dappy	bouncy
dekko	look
doan	don't
doings	an unspecified object, a whatsit
dout	put out, extinguish
dree	three
droo	through
drow	throw
duss	from the verb 'to do'; I do, thee duss
dussunt	do not
dyud	dead
ern	either
ex	ask
feow	few
fer	for
feyther	father
fower	four
frail	a small canvas bag
gaust	gorse
gurt	great or big
gwain	going
gyule	sneer
hommocks	legs
jadder	liar
ketch	catch
kip	keep
knaw	know
martal	mortal

muv	move
nern	none, neither
nogman	stupid person
ockerd	awkward
oik	lift, throw
olt	hold
on'n	of him or of it
on't	of it
on y'	of you
on us	of us
oot	will you
ootn't	won't you
ouja	an unspecified object, a whatsit
owd	hold
owld or ow'	old, often used in an affectionate way
phizog	face
pooer	poor
putt	put
quat or quatty	squat, crouch
sh'ink	should think
'sknaw	short for 'theesknaw' you know
smot	to throw, to hit, to break
smot up	dirty, as to be smot up with dirt
spitter	spade
squap	to tread or lean unevenly

sturt	startle
stwun	stone
summat	something
swelp my bob	an exclamation
teel	to stack or set
theesknaw	you know
theze	this
thic	that
thouse	you have
tripehound	silly person, a cur
tudjamler	tadpole, or any small fish
tuffut	turf
tush	pull, tug
'twunt	it won't
'tyunt	it isn't
ull	will
veel	feel
vire	fire
vit	feet
volla	follow
vorrud	forward or forehead
vust	first
vyarn	fern
vyow	few
watty-handed	cack handed, clumsy
wayter	water
wazzle	tangle
wesh	wash

wiffle	stink
witter	throw
wik	week
woy	way
wum	home
wunt or wun'	won't
wurrut	worry
yud	head
'yunt or 'yun'	see 'byunt'
yup	heap, many, much
yut	eat or eaten
youer	your
zurree	an exclamatory form of address